← Amguid ↓ Temouzared ↓ East ↓ Garet el Djenoun, 2330m ↓ Teffedest massif

The Nobility of
WILDERNESS

TRAVELS IN ALGERIA

Tom Sheppard

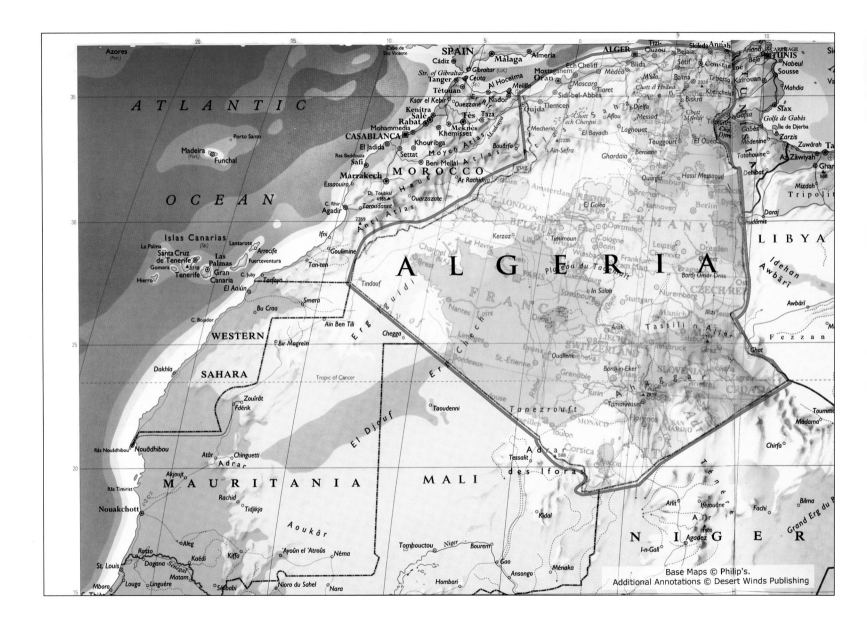

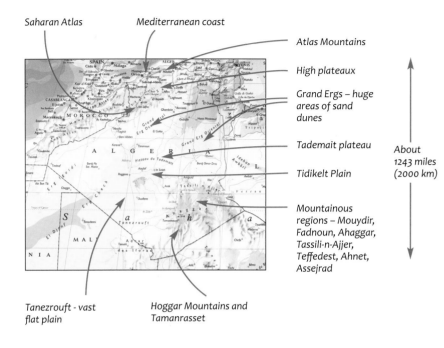

Saharan Atlas

Mediterranean coast

Atlas Mountains

High plateaux

Grand Ergs – huge
areas of sand
dunes

Tademait plateau

Tidikelt Plain

About
1243 miles
(2000 km)

Mountainous
regions – Mouydir,
Fadnoun, Ahaggar,
Tassili-n-Ajjer,
Teffedest, Ahnet,
Assejrad

Tanezrouft - vast
flat plain

Hoggar Mountains and
Tamanrasset

First this

Algeria is a very large country. I love its space and landscapes. Its landscapes are addictive. Though this immense and beautiful land is seemingly invisible to the UK media, it is, as the map opposite shows, bigger than Western Europe.

But if this book caught your eye, you'll probably already have an interest in Algeria and an awareness of the precious unspoilt wilderness to which it is host. A moon-view of the country's structure, however (near left), is worth sumarising. From the top down, there is the Mediterranean coastal strip, the Atlas (peaks 1500-2000m); the *Hautes Plateaux* averaging 700-1000m and the Saharan Atlas topping 1500m. Then, after skimming south over the vast dunescapes of the Grand Ergs, a flattish strip before the bleak Tademait plateau and a further dip to the Tidikelt plain where In Salah takes the brunt of the spring winds and sand storms. South of the Tidikelt the rock outcrops, hills and mountains emerge among the sand and gravel plains of the Sahara – majestic, noble landscapes and a perennial stop-and-think primer in geomorphology. Tahat's peak in the Hoggar rises to a height of 2908m.

North to south, Algeria covers nearly 18 degrees of latitude. At 60 nautical miles to the degree, that makes around 1240 statute miles or just about 2000km. In 2007 the UN-quoted population was 33.9 million.

When you contemplate a country the size of Algeria, the sheer dimensions and space of its wilderness, you soon find yourself wondering too about settlements and access – cities, terrain, roads, tracks, transport. Where do the people live? How do they get about? If you fill up with diesel in Tamanrasset, how did they get it there? Fresh fish, wet and silvery in the dusty beams of sunlight streaming into the covered market in Timimoun ... salmon cutlets a surprise choice on the dinner menu at In Salah's hotel? Astonishing.

So to get the feel of Algeria, and the wilderness-context of the book, there is a little, first, on the non-wilderness: the places against which to compare the magnificence of the remote areas. A visual swoop through a few of the human bolt-holes, the towns and distant communities. Then a glimpse of some of the people I was privileged to meet. And the setting: transport, communication; and the trees, water, weather – the influences and tools that create, nurture and perfect the wonder of the wild places.

To clarify it further, I have included towards the end of the book (p.228) a little on how I travelled – the faithful white Mercedes G-Wagen that appears in many of the photographs. And how I made my way around this exhilarating country, immersed in the unique beauty and the dignity of its landscapes. Some of the pictures are 30 years old (and, scanned from film, a few showing the limits of their tonal range) but most were gathered over an eight year period in which I was able to make six expeditions to the remotest regions in the Algerian Sahara.

I travelled in solitude, awe, wonder and supreme contentment, spiritually and mentally uplifted, feeling sometimes like the first man on earth, utterly at peace. The Sahara: sufficiently stern to keep all but the most appreciative at bay. For now, unspoiled by man's casual degradation of his environment through the tyranny of excess, greed, acquisition and the mindless, growth of population. Here, where less is so much more, in a land hewn by wind, weather and the almost ungraspable sculpture of geomorphology and time itself.

This wilderness must be protected and preserved – (p.233).

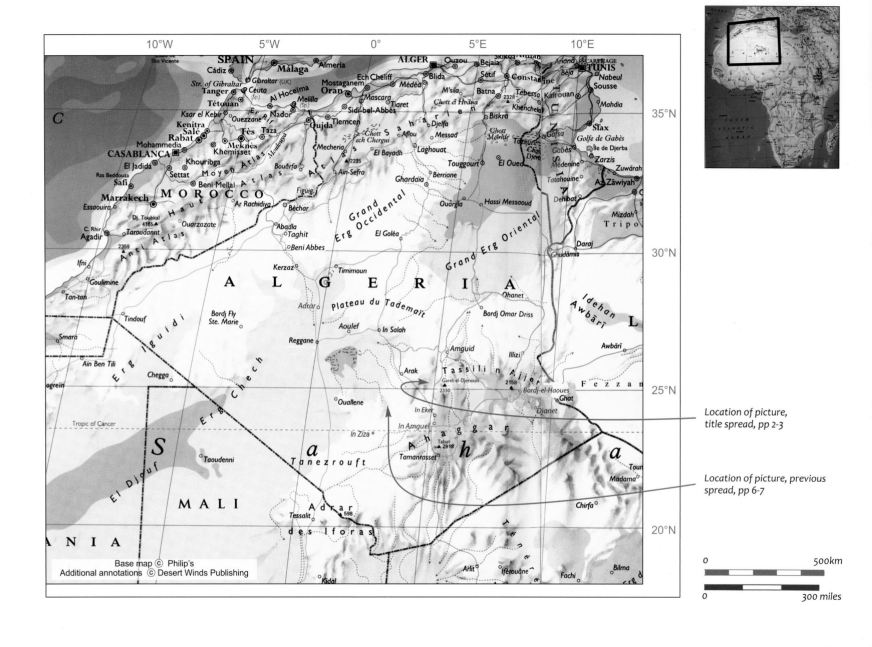

*Location of picture,
title spread, pp 2-3*

*Location of picture, previous
spread, pp 6-7*

Base map © Philip's
Additional annotations © Desert Winds Publishing

0   500km

0   300 miles

Contents

Preliminaries   4-7

    Contents   9

Non-wilderness:

    Towns

        Algiers   10

            Algiers Casbah   14

        Oran   19

        Up country   22

    People   34

    Transport   44

The setting:

    Weather and water   59

    Trees   81

Wilderness: 90

    Gour Rouhala   94

    Erg Mehedjebat   98

    Erg Telachchimt   100

    Sil Edrar   106

    Peak 1532   110

    Hahoumered   112

    Garet el Djenoun - 'GEDJ'   116

        GEDJ's realm, Teffedest, Izerane-n-Tirzi   118

        GEDJ's realm, Tidikmar   122

        GEDJ's realm, Temouzared   128

        GEDJ's realm, west   130

        GEDJ's realm, east   132

        GEDJ's realm, south   134

    Sun and moon   136

    Far west   146

    West – Hihaou, Nahalet   152

    South-west – Tiouiine   156

    South – Hoggar   158

    Adrar Ahnet   164

    West of Adrar Ahnet   166

    East of Adrar Ahnet   168

    South-east of Ahnet – Issedienne   180

    East of Ahnet – Tesnou   186

Interlude: fractals – a personal journey   202

Protected area – *L'espace des paysages*   233

The five-star, cavernous Aurassi Hotel, mischievously nick-named by Algerois 'le climatisseur' (the air conditioner: its blocky appearance – see p.14 – explains why) affords breathtaking views east over the harbour and coastal areas of Algiers.
Floodlit at night, the Monument des Martyrs (below and left, distant) is an imposing memorial to the war for independence – see also p.18. No wilderness this, except for the challenge of navigating the city's complex winding streets.
Artfully combining colonial French and Muslim architectural styles, the Grande Poste (right) dominates the square flanked by the Avenue Mohammed Khemisti.

Non-wilderness

Towns – Algiers

Algiers. *Alger la blanche,* as it has been called – a reference to the blinding white colour of the buildings that rim the shore when viewed from an approaching ship. The ever-expanding city sits in the 10km hollow of a bay spanning 15km east-west, a natural shelter from rough seas. With metros, tunnels, and dual carriageways attempting to ward off strangulation from its own development – and streets laid down before such pressures existed, Algiers pulses with energy – and people – day and night.

11

A trading post in the time of the Phoenicians, the existence of Algiers – El Djazair – dates back a thousand years. First a base for pirates and later government-backed privateers, it flourished from the mid 1500s for three centuries. Where others had failed, the French broke the grip of the sea-based pillage, taking the town peacefully in 1830 to establish a colonial rule that would last 132 years and end in horror. But they defined Algeria's borders, set up an administration and infrastructure. Algiers: now draped across hills stretching back 10km from the coast, serpentine roads easing traffic up the otherwise impossible gradients. The city extends 15km to the east to take in an airport, industrial zones and autoroutes.

Rue Emir el Khettabi (opposite), blue-balconied, white facaded, and an elegant legacy of French 19th century development, is a continuance of the main shopping street of the capital. Parc de la Liberté (left), with its own winding pathways, offers solitude for a young lady among the hurly-burly of Algiers' frenetic traffic.

'Le Climatisseur'
(Aurassi hotel, left)
faces south-east. This
is the back.
Straddling history
and the intervening
Casbah, about one-
and-a-quarter
kilometres behind me
as I took the picture,
is (below) the
mosquée des
Pêcheurs, the
fishermens' mosque
built in 1660. Nearby
in the Casbah, the
Ketchaoua Mosque
(right) was formerly
the Cathérdrale St
Phillipe, built on the
site on the original
mosque in the mid 19th century, and
reverted, in 1962, to Moslem use.
Algerian bakers have a rare expertise
with baguettes.

Built to mark colonial presence 1830-1930, the House of the Century *(left)* is a beautiful example of traditional architectural style. The Casbah is the old city. It is what the French would have seen in 1830 and built out from to make the present capital. Residents must the fittest people on earth – *(right)* especially with the extra payload on a family outing. Renovators are slowly gaining ground – the Bir Chebana drinking fountain *(below)* looking 21st-century pristine.

15

Huge brass trays for traditional feasts demand the most painstaking craftsmanship. The art of doing this (right) without producing a warped piece of scrap metal is clearly as specialised as producing the designs by eye. Tolerant neighbours – or plenty of earplugs – is obviously another feature of life in the Casbah.

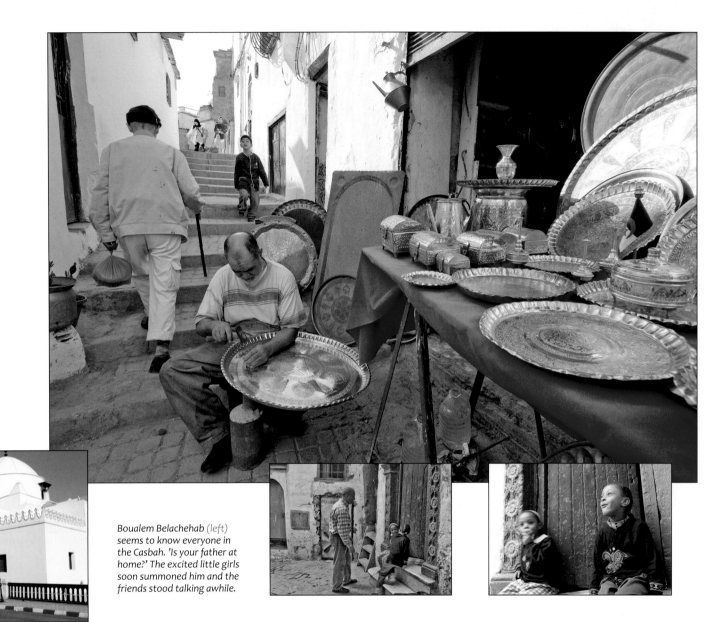

Boualem Belachehab (left) seems to know everyone in the Casbah. 'Is your father at home?' The excited little girls soon summoned him and the friends stood talking awhile.

Mutual support, as well as being one of the tenets of Arab family values, seems to apply to the survival of the Casbah's old buildings too *(left)*. The tiny Sidi Abdellah mosque *(right)* dates from Ottoman times – the lad on broom duty with the red (England) shirt is a little younger. Despite high national unemployment figures, industry and enterprise is the default. How early did the keeper of this patisserie *(below, centre)* get up to produce this display? Old soldiers, though, have time to sit and gossip.

Sombre reminders of the war for independence that raged between 1954 and 1962 at a terrible cost in lives and human misery. The French passion to retain the colony was just as understandable as the Algerians' wish that it should be theirs. Ali La Pointe, folk hero of the war, died with his son at this Casbah building *(right)*. The soaring Monument des Martyrs *(above)* is also the site of a deeply moving war museum.

Towns – Oran

Oran, second city and major gateway to Algeria, historically played second fiddle to Tlemcen for which it was the port but, without the Atlas in the way, provided easy access to the south. In modern times the oil and gas terminal of nearby Arzew has spawned industrial spin-off.

No less than in Algiers, the French architectural influence in Oran is startling. The form and ornamentation of the opera house, built in 1906, has you wondering where you are.

Oran's Cathédrale du Sacré-Coeur *(above)* in
the Place de la Kahina, built in 1931, makes a
notable contrast to the Mosquée du Pacha or
Grande Mosque *(right)* that dates from 1796.
Graffiti proclaims local political effort.

Oran's 19th century French town planning could not foretell future developments. Traffic density and the concomitant maze of one-way streets is frightening for the visitor. Grandiose architecture in what is now Place du 1 Novembre 1954, commemorating the start of the war for independence, remains a monument to colonial aspirations and arrogance. From claustrophobic streets the true wilderness calls.

Traditionally dressed or fully emancipated – women's apparel (left) is a fair indicator of the liberal approach to personal freedoms in Algeria.

Smooth barked eucalyptus (right), another of nature's miracles, seeming to thrive on impossibly dry sand.

Ain Sefra (above) guards the southern fringes of the high plateau, a dusty town starting to get more of a wilderness feel about it – rocky hills to the north, sand dunes crowding the Mehkta Hotel on the south edge of town but kept at bay by giant eucalyptus trees.

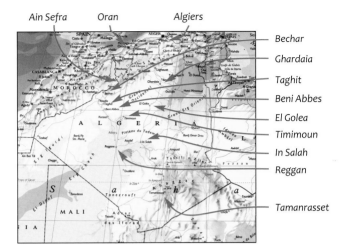

Ain Sefra   Oran   Algiers

Bechar

Ghardaia

Taghit

Beni Abbes

El Golea

Timimoun

In Salah

Reggan

Tamanrasset

Towns recap – **see also** *larger map on p.8*

Towns – up-country

Taghit is a tiny gem of a town – more of a village – on a minor road that enables you to by-pass the choking industry of Bechar. Simple, small and well kept, Taghit sits by a palmerie on the edge of the Oued Zousfana and defies the vast sands of the Grand Erg Occidental that stretch more than 200 miles to the east.

Taghit (right) *with its neat hotel designed by the charismatic architect Fernand Pouillon* (above) *hosts rock art* (left) *of extraordinary durability. Exposed to the elements for thousands of years, the look is of carving completed the previous week.*

23

Ibadites of the strict Kharijite sect, driven from Tahert by orthodox Muslims, settled in the Oued Mzab a thousand years ago. Now a five-town group centred on Ghardaia (left), the Mozabites are still almost a country within a country, its people characterised by a special energy and commercial flair. Extensive palmeries support gardens for vegetable produce. The valley is vulnerable to serious flooding when the infrequent rains come.

El Golea (above), like Ghardaia, is noted for its palm groves and vegetable gardens. Once an important staging post on the southbound caravan routes, it now also produces bottled drinking water exported throughout the region. The remains of Father Charles de Foucauld, a pivotal figure in the pacification of the Sahara region during early colonisation, are interred beside a memorial church built in 1929. (See also p.26)

Towns – Ghardaia, El Golea

Ghardaia (opposite) and El Golea (above), respectively about 300 and 450 miles south of Algiers (map previous spread), sit beside the north-south route to Tamanrasset. In recent years El Golea was renamed El Meniaa – after the crumbling fortress from which this picture (above) was taken.

Some 200 miles west of El Golea, over the Grand Erg, Beni Abbes, like Taghit, is blessed with palm groves. It perches on the banks of the Oued Saoura *(opposite)* which can swell to a swirling torrent when the rains come. The fort was built by the French as was the museum and centre for Saharan research *(below)*, now somewhat neglected. Father Charles de Foucauld, missionary, diplomat, peacemaker and part-architect of Algeria in the 19th century, built his first hermitage here in 1901 – preserved to this day *(below right)* by followers of the brotherhood.

The south-western gateway to Timimoun is through the Porte du Soudan (left) *– an immaculate example of the puddled red clay finish to buildings in this part of the Gourara and Timimoun in particular. The wide main street* (right) *bears signs of French influence but the architectural style remains – even in the beehive form of the marabout tombs.*
The palmeries run alongside the sebkha (salt marsh) but are irrigated through ingenious underground conduits (fogarras) that terminate in intricate dividing channels (below) *to each plot or tree.*
Timimoun is a long way (lower right) *from neighbouring towns.*

Towns – Timimoun

There is something special about Timimoun – even in the sonorous nature of the name. A kind of tranquillity and integrity and being content to be what it is reflected in the attitude and kindness of the people who live there. A recent nearby gas-field discovery will bring a commercial boost but, hopefully, not spoil the ambience of Timimoun.

The clay plasterwork in the building's interior (above and right) is astonishing in its intricacy and variety – and all done by eye without the aid of drawings or other design templates. The sheer love of craftsmanship shines through.

A unique building on Timimoun's main street started as the Hotel Atlantique in 1926. Opened and patronised by the Grand Duchess of Luxembourg on a flying visit, it later became the Hotel Rouge and is now the town's Cultural Centre. Director Djouiber Mansoor is an impressionist artist as well as being the embodiment of Timimoun calm, hospitality and generosity.

Muslims fast between dawn and dusk for Ramadan which marks the month in which the Qur'an was revealed to the Prophet Mohammed. The Eid al-Fitr festival takes place at the end of Ramadan and is usually a four-day holiday, celebrated with feasting. Tribal celebration often takes the form of displays such as this (left) – the 'fête' in the village of Oulad Said near Timimoun.

The muskets (below) are very old, often muzzle-loaded with gunpowder and are discharged, deafeningly and in unison, at the conclusion of the dance ceremony. The flag represents the sheikh of the region in which the celebration takes place. Jeans and trainers at ground level connect with the 21st century.

(Opposite) Evening stroll, Timimoun.

People

I wondered if it was just me, with rose-tinted spectacles. But I found comfort and justification on reading my precious, old and well-respected Nagel's guidebook – written when guidebooks were put together by mature and qualified people – that their observation on Algerians was very much in accord with my own. After listing individuals from guides to waiters, to booksellers, to landladies, Nagel observes: 'All of them have shown a friendliness and helpfulness which the authors ... have rarely found equalled in any other country.'

And: 'Whether (the visitor) is dealing with a taxi driver, a student of progressive ideas, a civil servant in Algiers, one of the village elders in some remote part of the country or the ordinary man in the street in one of the towns, he will find everywhere the same eagerness to express in concrete form the traditional hospitality of the Arab.'

When I took the picture of the Grande Poste (on p.11), I was approached by one of the booksellers who welcomed me to Algiers and shared my joke that the building's twin domes were oddly reminiscent of the old Wembley Stadium.

In Timimoun, seeking to buy some eggs and biscuits in a small shop and not having the right money, I offered a high denomination note. The shopkeeper had no change but, after no more than a couple of seconds' thought said, 'Well, take it anyway.' On my solo journeys in remote areas encounters with rightly cautious soldiers on patrol (next spread) are not uncommon. Invariably it is quickly a case of changing the grip on the rifle to smile and shake hands.

(Below) El Golea. His family with (centre) Abdelkarim who took time out to show me the town and then asked me to a meal at his home. I had met him in the street and just asked the way to the old fort.

(Upper right) Tamanrasset. Younes, eight years old, proves his Touareg lineage. The camel is patient and supremely capable but knows who's boss.

(Right, main picture) In Amenas. A kindly pause by the workers at the gas collection project to accommodate my request for a photograph of engineering on such a massive scale.

(Left) Inspection and document checks done, as duty dictates for a lone vehicle found out in the desert, joshing and mutual picture-taking was then in order. The Algerian army was always on the ball, good humoured and good company.

(Above) The remote well at Tabelbalet was a watering hole for their thirsty herd and a great deal of hard work for the Touareg pulling ropes. One had bleeding hands from the repetitive toil but, with his colleague, summoned a smile for the camera.

(Right) Full-time, professional coffee-drinkers and white-plastic chair test pilots get some serious business done in Laghouat – a scene repeated a thousand times on any sunny morning in Algeria where news is important.

At In Salah a 'delegation' groups at an office for 'discussions'. Development of the nearby 'Ahnet' gas field will hopefully invigorate InSalah's economy and provide jobs, but the serious business of buying fresh bread in the market, still warm from the ovens across the way, is not affected.

Tipasa's near-empty Hotel de Baie has a wide beach (left). Devoid of visitors, it affords ample space for the young fishermen to bring home the supper. At the Teguentur gas plant, north of In Salah, (below) the work goes on.

A congested world away from In Salah – or 750 miles north (left) – young Algerois disport themselves. A poseur who has seen too many fashion ads; sparky little girls, and young boys – already style-conscious too – mimic victory signs, each face a window to the tentative personality within.

A lone Touareg at remote Ain al Hadjadj, 70 miles west of Illizi, draws water (left). A hundred and fifty miles south-west, a day's camel ride out of Amguid, (right) a chance encounter in the blowing dust is an opportunity to shake hands, admire the camels and exchange greetings.

A Michael Palin film rolls in the Hoggar (above) – Nigel Meakin at the camera, son Peter behind while John Pritchard monitors sound. And where in the Sahara (right) do you not encounter German bikers on tall Wagnerian motorcycles – here being educated to the delights of English tea?

Tamanrasset's tranquil ambience (right) masks go-ahead expansion. Highly original new houses, neat and attractive, flank the approach road into town – one new owner happy to display his new domain for a curious visitor. More remarkable still, a university is taking shape nearby – with extravagant Touareg architectural motifs.

Competing with Ghardaia's established reputation, production of rugs and tapestries (left) is one of El Golea's busy industries. Seeing the girls were shy I hesitated to take pictures but Madame Directeur's calm stilled the giggling without interrupting production.

Himself and his beautiful white camel (above), on solo walkabout – like me – around 70 miles southwest of Arak near Idjenoudjane. An amazing pair; the boy can't have been more than 17. I would have given anything to be able to talk at length. Near Tadjemout, on the Arak old road, (left) this Touareg had seen it all.

Transport

When you talk about transport and roads in Algeria you think of the country's size – bigger than Western Europe (maps on pp.4 and 8). The distances, the engineering task, are jaw-dropping. Then you add the climatic extremes. Roads built to carefully judged criteria are suddenly, due to violent rain or floods, found to be outside the parameters. In some areas there are just tracks. Often, where you need to go there are not even tracks.

On the tarmac, a lone fuel tanker (left), *carrying the life-blood of the country, drops down off the plateau and heads south past the giant dune just north of Kerzaz. The Oued Saoura, at the foot of the distant ridge, can turn into a voracious destroyer when the heavy rains rumble down from Morocco* (see also p.76). *Near Arak* (below) *heavy rain has already done its work.*

In the north of Algeria the road engineers' problems were different but their persistence and skill prevailed. Safety hazards (upper right) are unique to the region. Some routes (right), no more than a dotted line on (old) maps, are even more tentative on the ground. With the right sun angle, you might get lucky and see where others have been – a long time ago. Others (opposite) like the old RN1, are easier and still bear the distance markers.

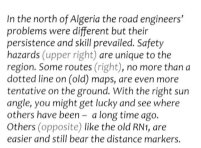

Heavies (above) approaching the 400km stretch of the Tademait Plateau between El Golea and In Salah – hours of tedium, now at least a sealed road and cured of the choking, powder-fine dust of former years. Usually (left) a convoy assembles at El Golea for security reasons – but not always.

The Fadnoun plateau (right and upper right) is possibly the most implacably hostile landscape for transport in all Algeria. The route has only recently been tarmacked. Think about that: 270 kilometres on severely corrugated, almost raw terrain south from Illizi. A test to destruction for many vehicles.

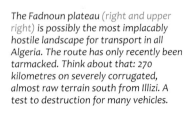

The original route – roughly 750km – from Ouargla (map p.8) in the north-east to In Salah, followed the oueds and wells along the way, taking in such places as the old fort at Ain Guettara (below). The advent of long-range vehicles made the bleak and hostile Tademait plateau an attractive alternative. The Tademait is relatively smooth but ends in a precipitous escarpment at its southern edge. Enter – again – the audacious road engineers who carved a breathtaking zigzag down the cliff faces at Ain al Hadjadj (right) and then slotted a road into the existing oueds. Still heading south, it crosses a further modest plateau, descends a small scarp down onto the Tidikelt Plain and eventually reaches In Salah. Ain Guettara and the many old tracks are still patrolled by the Algerian army on the lookout for bandits and smugglers.

If the wadi floods are especially energetic – which is most of the time – they will undermine and collapse the hard-won smoothness of the tarmac *(below)*. The trucks keep going where they can but sometimes *(right)* a diversion is necessary and the artics take to the gravel on the temporary routes. In the hills and wadis round Arak – as shown here – diversions and minor drama is the norm. Between Ghardaia and El Golea *(opposite)* life is lonely but a little more predictable.

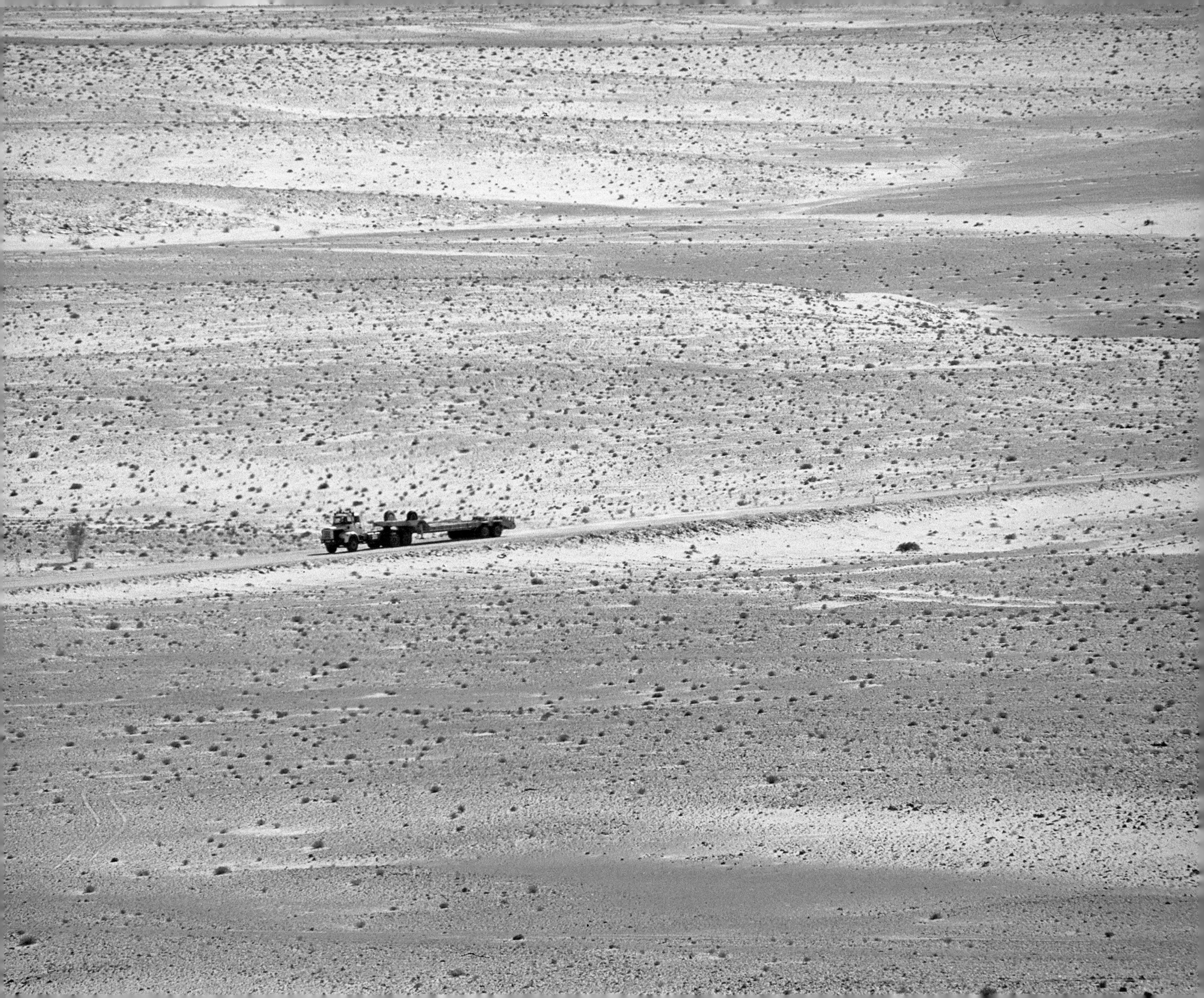

Nature's own speed bumps *(left)* – or rather speed monitors, since there is an optimum, rather than just a maximum speed at which to drive over them. The old RN1, shown here in the main picture, was the principal north-south route to Tamanrasset and followed the line of water points and oases between In Salah and Arak. The new tarmac road, strangely, is 'out in the desert' to the west, easier to survey but seemingly – and surprisingly – more vulnerable to flood damage. Whilst the old RN1 was cairned and, in its day graded, navigating the disused Djanet-Amguid track *(right)* is left to intuition, an intermittent profusion of tracks and an iron post – a legacy of the past.

French-era benchmarks *(left)* bearing the Institut Géographique Nationale 1955 imprint, often found even on the most remote routes together with hilltop cairns, are reassuring to encounter. On other routes, if that is an appropriate term *(right)*, you may surmise that perhaps there hasn't been much recent traffic.

Mechanical transport, off-road, sometimes adapts with difficulty when conditions are a little ... too wet ... too dry ... too hard ... or too soft ...

... but there's another type of transport (opposite) – highly versatile – for whom it is all in a day's work. The Touareg referred to his camels as 'Mes quatre-quatres!' (My four-by-fours.)

The human interface with a vast country like Algeria is dependent on transport: getting about in order to see it, to benefit from it, to cultivate and industrialise it in the north, to soak up its space and beauty in the south and support remote towns and villages.

It is impossible not to hold in enormous respect the Touareg who live in the wilderness in such harmony that their camels provide most of the transport they need. The ingredients of effective transport where larger population has to be supported in the 21st century are vehicles of rugged build and off-road capability, roads, tracks and the provision of fuel.

Constantly developed since, the French period of colonisation laid an extraordinary foundation of routes for wheeled vehicles. The In Salah-Amguid route over the rocky heights of Idjarane *(left)* is a typical example of engineering audacity and logistical capability.

SNTR *(below)* transports fuel to Algeria's most distant settlements even when the tarmac is out of commission.

The setting

Weather and water

Just as the popular perception of the Sahara as a vast region of sand dunes is a myth, so also is the idea of endless burning sunshine from a merciless glowing disc vertically overhead. Certainly sun is the norm. But there is strong wind and there is vigorous rain from time to time. In a region with virtually no topsoil to absorb it, surprisingly frequent heavy rain falling on bare rocky hills has nowhere to go but quickly down into wadis and low-lying areas. These fill and the floods tear into man-made structures such as road foundations – see p.52. The feel of nature's brute energy, however, is exhilarating – if heartbreaking for the engineers trying to keep the national infrastructure functioning (see p.62). Increasingly, even off-tracks in the remote areas, significant attention must be paid to surface water (p.56, top left) or – more dangerous because of its invisibility – that which lurks beneath (p.62). To the Touareg, of course (p.62 again) topping up the water bags then means less digging. And they're good at knowing precisely where to dig.

As meteorological statistics confirm, In Salah, *(map, p.8)* with its seemingly endless north-east winds *(above)* has the edge on just about anywhere else in the Sahara for dust storms. It has trophies to show for it even when the wind drops – *upper centre picture on p.46.* Other areas, though, such as the Oued Tirit *(left)* on the old track west from Amguid, can still summon a suitably sinister gloom when the conditions are right. An eerie magnificence, hinting at the power of the elements and the insignificance of man, seems to prevail. Appropriately, the local name is Meskem el Djenoun which translates loosely as Dwelling of the Spirits.

Enough to make the road engineers weep. Floods have torn the road apart, culverts designed to channel the water have been brushed aside and by-passed. The precious green optical cable linking Tamanrasset with the north is bared. And elsewhere, a wadi's seemingly dry surface (upper right) conceals dangerously soft ground to snare a vehicle.

Wondrously in harmony with their environment, (right) a Touareg group decide, on their way to Issedienne, that it is time to let the camels have a snack while they attend to the logistics. This may be the last water for a while. There has been a little rain recently and the Oued Tekchouli will have something to offer. These men know where to dig in order to fill their water containers. A wristwatch, stylish sunglasses and clothes ideal for the climate – all town-bought: they still prefer their desert way of life. The Oued Tekchouli can summon awesome power (next page) when in spate, dislodging whole trees.

Not much grows on rocks. Certainly not trees this size *(left)*. In flood with water from the Hoggar, Oued Tekchouli, it seems, uprooted the trunk and sent it far up onto a rock island on the crest of a bow wave as the torrent roared out into the Afedafed flood plain.

Here in calmer mood, Tekchouli retains shallow pools *(above)* of which fresh grasses are quick to take advantage. Two hundred miles north, on the old Amguid track, recent rain *(right)* fosters the flowering of robust bushes, thorned and armoured against climate and wildlife.

65

This (right) is weather, not water, at Adrar Idjerane on the old Amguid track – rays of the sun split by the clouds lighting up the dust particles in the air. But east of here at Oued Askef – the first alarming indication being the wicked glint of water among the grass mounds – (far left), the rain has made the two kilometre wide water-course a dangerously uncrossable barrier that demanded a 50 km detour (upper left). Moderate rain on flat ground just forms puddles that finally dry out (below centre) but leach the fine clays to the surface in cracked flakes, ingredients for the next dust storm ... rather like the airborne fine sand hiding the massif of Tourmourine, west of Amguid (below) or (p.71) the peaks of Tidikmar.

Late afternoon winds refine the geo-
sculpture that nature has been working on
for some time – a daily miracle related to
critical wind speed, sand-grain size ...

... and the magic of illumination. Job done, calm air and dawn light display an exquisite form; a combination of simplicity and complexity to inspire even M Bézier.

Vigorous rearrangement of the landscape in progress *(right) as the wind rushes the slope of a big dune 40 miles north of In Ziza (p.74), furiously flying over the edge and taking the sand with it in the turbulence. Beautifully conceived homesteads (below) at Alya, north-east of Ghardaia, can sadly be consumed by changing weather patterns and climate over the years.*

Part-caused, paradoxically, by rain that *(lower centre picture, p.66) brings fine clays to the surface to dry out, the broad plain north-west of the Teffedest massif seems to be specially prone to 'storms' of fine dust – here (right) spoiling Tidikmar's grandeur – better seen on p.122 et seq.*

One wall of Arak's precipitous cliffs reflects the soft glow from the other *(left)* where the spectacular gorge is shared by road and oued. The co-existence works well here but a kilometre or so west *(see p.52)* the water has won the day comprehensively. Arak *(map p.8)* traps and re-radiates the heat like a year-round oven. In heavy rain the place is victim of the floods' force that regularly repositions the road. Forty miles south, the water plays tranquil mirror *(above)* in Swan Lake mode.

Nature provides, as well as being playful with man's little creations such as roads. The guelta (rock pool) at In Ziza *(main picture, left and map p.8)* is about 310 kilometres north-west of Tamanrasset and a very long way from any other water source. Even more surprising is its location high among the rocks of Hihaou. Equally amazing – and munificent – is Ain Kahla *(lower left)*, an artesian well and constantly refreshed pool of clear water 130km east of in Salah. Coming over the vast blank gravel 700km from Bordj Omar Driss, the sight initially defies belief.

The guelta at Tiguelgamine is conveniently situated alongside the old route from Arak to In Salah – or maybe that should be the other way round! *(Above shows the upper pool that cascades into the main valley and outlet, left)* A hundred miles south of In Salah, this will have been a crucial watering place for southbound camel caravans and influenced placing of the original main Route National 1.

In the dry, the dust on the old Arak track rides the wind *(above)*, ghostly and wraith-like. When the rains hit hard in Morocco 400 miles north-west, the Oued Saoura *(left)* takes enormous amounts of water and channels it south. Kerzaz *(see p.44 and map, p.8)* sits beside the Grand Erg and the Saoura skirts the small settlement. Fifty miles to the south, the same flood water roars through 20 culverts *(below)* at Foum el Kheneg on the road to Adrar and Reggan; a new bridge, 30 miles north, nimbly built between flood events, spans the great wadi *(left)* at Erg Ogab – and kept the photographer's feet dry.

The weather and the water put on a show for me between In Eker and Arak. Raindrops that seemed each to have come from an eggcup, dark threatening sky, roiling curtains of rain and low cloud – and mercifully it had waited until I was on tarmac. Just 48 hours earlier I had been in the Oued Tekchouli where this much water would have put me in serious trouble (I thought of that tree trunk on p.64)). A small rainbow (right) seemed to be wishing me well and the water that formed a weir over the road (above) led away harmlessly into the desert to nourish the grasses.

With no water on hand to do it, the weather was
providing a mock lake. The high temperature was the
trigger for a mirage. Not a specially rare phenomenon and
it's only after you've looked at this one for a few
moments that you realise something is wrong. All
mirages, after all, are a reflection of what's above and are
thus upside down. Here, however, the reflection is the
right way up – an indication of a double mirage: a
reflection of a reflection on a second layer of heated air.

Trees

If it is surprising to find a section heading like this in a book on the Sahara it is even more surprising to see, and ponder, the trees themselves when you encounter them. Amazing enough to see trees at all but when you observe their size, their almost armour-plated robustness, their placing and spacing, and the refinement of their adaptation to the conditions, it is easy to become lost in wonder.

You find yourself asking why there is just one? One, that has grown to such height and strength? Trees are not like animals that fight for supremacy yet one seed of many, borne by the wind or by birds, has flourished, often to absolute perfection (see p.88).

And on closer inspection you find that each tree has its own little ecosystem – ants or other insects, birds nesting in the branches and feeding off the insects. There is shade for animals, as gazelle droppings attest. There is some forage for them too – but only so much; limited by the ferocity of the tree's thorns, the virtual impregnability of its armour, its height and the reach of a camel's neck.

Seeing this tree (left), I tried to break off a piece of bark to see how soft it might be. I think I now have a concept of what crushed titanium would feel like. No mouflon or gazelle would make much progress here.

If some trees *(p.81)* have iron bark, others *(left)* get by with subtly positioned thorns and a bark smooth enough to slough off the harsh desert winds. A solitary tree's glorious foliage *(below)*, high above camels' reach, glows a rich green against the sky among Tidikmar's dramatic peaks and promontories.

Part of the answer *(left)* to the questions raised on the previous page. The new trees come up where the most water will collect when it rains; Tininirt's classic cleft valley *(satellite picture next page)* provides the rain run-off. And they come up fighting, already bristling with thorns, just like the mature tree behind.

The smooth sweeping rock faces of Tininirt, *(facing page)* intriguingly red in the satellite shot *(left)* and emulating blackleaded cast iron in certain light *(upper left)* provide perfect run-off for rain. But again, just a single, special tree seems to take advantage. How deep are their roots? The same, next-to-the-massif principle seems to apply at peak 1532 *(above)*.

Side-lit by the setting sun at the foot of Garet el Djenoun near the north end of the Teffedest massif and showing the rich brown of its bark *(left)*, this acacia is a different type to the one on p.81. With this much run-off, a sprinkling of trees grow nearer the mountain but this one stands alone farther out on the plain.

This tree *(right)* beside the road north of Bordj el Haoues, clearly had a hard time early in its life but survived to produce a fine crown of foliage and shade for passing travellers. Beside nothing at all except a low distant outcrop near Aketeb , the lone acacia *(below)* seemed to celebrate its utter perfection with tiny white blossoms,

This magnificent, astonishing, robust, perfect, giant acacia (left), emerges cleanly from the ground near the Tesnou complex of outcrops. You long to know its age, its history, how deep are its roots, how it survived its early years when still vulnerable to grazing gazelle and camels. Elsewhere, (right), at Tiouiine, 150 miles south, a tree (nilotica acacia) spontaneously bleeds gum in the late autumn from its main branches, adhering to the trunk or falling to the ground. Traditionally it has nutritional and medicinal applications.

Wilderness

Landscape

Algeria's most memorable visual experiences are to be seen in the remote Sahara. Just as there must be night for there to be day and there must be non-wilderness (pages 10-21) to appreciate true wilderness, so there are parts of the Sahara (below left) that are plain – in both senses of the word. This scenic asceticism, arguably appropriate to the disciplines of life in the desert, is in some ways a wry spur to appreciation of visual events when they occur. It is a constant reminder, too, of scale; the sheer size of the Sahara is awe-inspiring, not only for its magnitude but for the variety of its landscape. The remainder of the book is devoted to just some of the majestic landscapes which are there for the careful, respectful and appreciative to see. I have proposed a Protected Area (p.233) that includes most of the locations portrayed here so that they may be preserved and enjoyed by – and only by – the careful, respectful and appreciative.

When mention is made of desert landscapes it's impossible not to think first of the grace and beauty of windblown sand formations. Jumping less readily to mind are images of sand and rock outcrop intermingling – geomorphology and the sculpture of the elements combined.

This almost hypnotic juxtaposition of form *(left)*, lies casually among the dunes south of *El Golea (see maps p.8 and 23)*, – a kind of visual yin and yang, a conundrum, that I look at and can never quite work out the principle of its symmetry. As if it's trying to test your powers of observation *(below)*, a perfect windblown curve peaks precisely at the dip of distant hills in the long dune band at *Telachchimt (see also p.100 et seq)*.

Unromantically dubbed
'Cmp 30/4' on my first visit,
I discovered from the
immaculately crafted
French IGN maps that this
wonderful place about 75
miles north of El Golea *(also
shown at sunset on p.91)*
has a name – Gour
Rouhala – and a busy
population. The rocks
protruding through the
sand dune *(above)*,
scorched by eons of sun
and cooled by the ensuing
night, had cracked to show
their displeasure.

At Gour Rouhala the light (left), turns a desiccating invasion into
beauty, enshrines the wind's subtle sculpture and the myriad sand
grain sizes to produce a delicate ripple to rival the harsh profile of
the mesas. Flare from the camera lens makes its contribution to the
composition of the image. Still at Rouhala, (above), a spirit-level
could have aligned the mesa tops. The invading sand gives way to
the sheer determination of plant life to survive.

The menacing mass of the Erg Mehedjebat dunes beside the Arak-In Salah road (facing page), loom an intimidating 250m above the surrounding desert – and give intruders some hard work (right) coping with the ultra-fine sand grains around its fringes. Sixty miles north-east the simplicity of a thin layer of sand (below), provides a palette to bear a vehicle's tracks in a graceful curve.

Erg Telachchimt's pure, pristine, untrodden undulations evoke a mystic aura, almost surreal – magical when seen in late afternoon light. A sinuous third dimension emerges in the perfection of detail after the harsh, flat, unrelenting glare of a midday sun overhead.

Erg Telachchimt: a serene band of creamy-coloured dunes watched over by the majestic distant, 2330m peak of Garet el Djenoun (p.116 and map p.8), to the south-west. If form were sound, this, for its variety and perfect detail, would surely be the quiet opening of a symphonic masterpiece.

The supreme privilege of being
at Erg Telachchimt around
sunset and – a little farther to
the east – when the moon rises
silently. The absence of drama
makes it all the more dramatic.

Sil Edrar, east of the road between Arak and In Eker *(map p.8)*, vies with the ragged peaks of Tesnou and Ezzouiague *(distant, left of the picture)*, for dramatic impact. A massif about eight kilometres square, this huge outcrop of solid unbroken rock could, with some justification, be labelled Algeria's Uluru – though its extent is far greater. Pondering its mass and thermal capacity, you have to wonder how it copes with the solar input of a June sun for 12 hours a day, and the cold of winter nights; what structural stresses build up and what temperature gradient exists through its crust. The tree and shrubs, of course, take advantage of the run-off when it rains.

Geomorphologists would have been reaching for their notebooks the day Sil Edrar popped up from underground (professionals say that isn't strictly how it happened). Spiky *(left)*, flat *(right)*, or split down the middle and eroded like praying hands *(below)*, there was a rock formation for everyone.

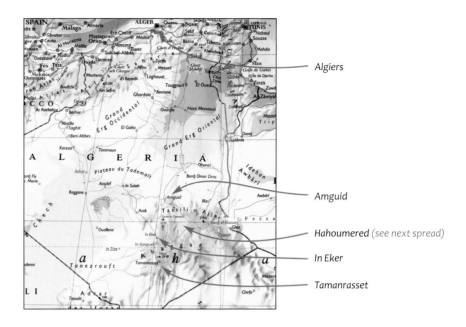

Algiers

Amguid

Hahoumered (see next spread)

In Eker

Tamanrasset

Somewhere, way off-tracks to the west of
the dusty route between the tiny
gendarmerie outposts at Amguid and In Eker,
across a shallow wadi, lies Peak 1532 – an
extraordinary, jagged massif on the skyline.
A dip in its profile leaves the impression of a
processional enfilade to a throne-room
where awaits, in the distance, the dignified,
effulgent presence of the Emperor Peak. In
fact, it is no more than a unique
juxtaposition of geological outcrops but the
effect is enough to stop you in your tracks –
particularly, as here, at sunset. Vangelis,
John Williams – or Wagner – could have
written some impressive film music to a
scene such as this.

'God's telephone dial!' Round outcrops arranged in a huge circle on the satellite picture and French IGN map (right) look just like that. One of them, Hahoumared, is also marked with a pick and shovel icon indicating its one-time importance as a source of salt – great slabs of it, 10 or 15 centimetres thick (left), that will have been transported to markets on camel-back. The high view (above), with visiting vehicles, shows the extent of the dried lake. Demanding access through immense landscapes, Its vivid portrayal on LandSat imagery and its remote location more than 100 kilometres from any regularly used road or track lend Hahoumared a special mystery and attraction.

*South of Hahoumered, looking south-west, a
jagged horizon of peaks scratches the
skyline, precursor to the monumental
outcrops of the Hoggar 150 miles farther on.*

Garet el Djenoun

If ever a mountain had a presence, a gravitas, a dignity, an authority, then surely it is Garet el Djenoun – 'GEDJ', 2330m (map, p.8 and next spread). No doubt, in naming it (the translation is Mountain of the Spirits) the traditional wanderers of the Sahara felt there was something special about it too. Heading the northern end of the Teffedest range, it seems to look out over its realm to the north, west and east, with regal mien, visible from miles around.

Seen from the north-east (left), Garet el Djenoun (GEDJ) can look, from a distance, like Durham Cathedral embedded in granite. Through a long lens, west, at midday it looks frightening (right).

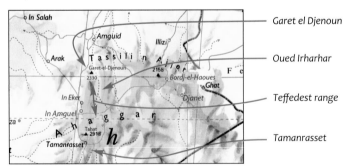

Garet el Djenoun

Oued Irharhar

Teffedest range

Tamanrasset

Impressive back-up. This view (above), looks south-west at the Teffedest massif with Peak 2214, some 12km south of Garet el Djenoun, to the right of the picture. In the foreground, its edge studded with shrubs, a long, narrow oued – the Oued Irharhar – stretches north-west to south-east but later heads south.

Conical mounds (right), the result of sand build-up around generations of vegetation growing and dying, lie still under the hegemony of Garet el Djenoun, away in the distance.

Izerane-n-Tirzi, an intriguing series of small outcrops only a couple of hundred metres above local ground level. Fifty kilometres north of Garet el Djenoun, in the centre of the wide Igharghar plain running down from Amguid, it manages, in true Saharan fashion, to provide a delightful scenic miniature for the traveller.

Tidikmar is easy of access and lies beside the Amguid-In Eker track (map p.118) – mischievously, almost exactly on the 25° N line of latitude where one map sheet joins the next. But it is worth the cab-filling, crackling cacophony of unwieldy map sheets to wander among its crisp sand formations and Dali-esque peaks. These little ridges, (left), however, artistically sculpted by the wind, are rock-hard and will get a vehicle airborne if its driver has not seen them in time to slow down. With a high sun they are almost impossible to see.

Here looking pristine and razor sharp, Tidikmar is no less prone to the weather's capriciousness than any other location – (see p.71),

Deep blue sky illuminates the shaded areas of Tidikmar's sandy slopes *(right)*, to give them an unreal hue while the sun goes down. The sand is sugar-crust crisp underfoot and almost as firm as concrete under the wheels of a four-by-four. Wheel tracks are quickly tidied away by the wind – even the explorer's joke meeting *(above)*: 'Doctor Livingstone, I presume!'

A pre-dawn prelude *(above)*, and the fanfare of the sun appearing at Tidikmar *(right)*, is an inspiring experience. The magic scenic ingredient, the sun, its angle, its timing, the kind of sky it shines from – is as well displayed at Tidikmar as anywhere in the Sahara. Better, though, for the stark silhouettes of the peaks, the textures of the rock looming out of the shadows, and the sweeping curves of the small sand ridges that the wind, curling round the outcrops, so beautifully creates.

North-west of Tidikmar, groups of outcrops dot the Igharghar plain still within distant sight of Garet el Djenoun. Each, as you take in the beauty of smaller and smaller gems of landscape – *see 'Fractals', p.202* – supports its own unique features. Here *(left)*, coming from the west, an incline between the two hills leads suddenly to this perfect arc of sand that the wind has laid across the gap. An immaculately curved wind-hollow *(above)*, beside a rock bears tracks of a tiny adventurous lizard.

Sand is an unlikely medium for sculpture, yet time and again in the Sahara, the pure, graceful profiles, the textures and – as here – the delicate subtlety of colour, leave you gazing in wonder at the sheer perfection of it all. Some 60km north-west of Garet el Djenoun, this rare formation, overlaid with buttresses of cream-coloured sand, fringes the plain before the terrain gives way to the Mouydir Mountain massif to the north.

Aheggar (opposite), is a mighty outcrop running parallel to the Teffedest range, its sheer scale emphasised by the fact that it is isolated – and around 16km long. It is, you feel, here to stay. Farther east still (left), with lighting to make Caravaggio weep, clean translucent rocks face the declining sun and (above), a gentle valley looks south over a vast plain where the Tamanrasset-Djanet track meanders eastwards.

133

The southern end of the Teffedest is a wild riot of mountains, ridges and outcrops fringing a wide notional east-west valley separating it from the Ahaggar mountains to the south *(map p.118)*. Delicately split by the tendrils of sandy valleys, wadis and a thin network of tracks, it is 120km or more south of Garet el Djenoun yet somehow, with its lesser peaks, bows to the great mountain's dominance.

Sun and moon

'The alchemy of light' is a phrase I have used before but fits like no other the magic wrought by the ever-changing position, angle and intensity of the sun and moon over desert wilderness. The pure forms that nature, with its millennia of erosion, wind and geomorphology have created – and those forms too that seem to have resulted from chaos and upheaval – respond with elegance or sheer drama to the changing source, slant and colour of the light. The mood can vary: the harsh, hostile glare of midday, the long, gentle graded shadows of sunset or the vivid expectant glow of pre-dawn. Then again, there's sunrise itself ... .

I sometimes thought the sun had its very own sense of drama. 'How about this then?', it seems to be saying. I had to smile.

Even when the terrain is, as it were, relaxed, the sun and moon can provide breath-catching visual excitement. Flat, rolling gravelly plain some way to the south east of Ain al Hadjadj (see p.51), is enlivened by a sultry dawn and purple sky. As if putting on a show for the Eid new moon that marks the end of the Ramadan month of fasting, the lunar event includes a clear view of the shaded side. And when that moon becomes full, the light it sheds (above), is almost theatrical.

139

The sun, pre-dawn west of Tazat's 2061m double peaks south-west of Zaouatallaz *(near right)*, and at sunset on the dunes south of El Golea *(below)*, brings colour and perfect gradation to the skies – and a third dimension to the desert. Around 250 miles west of Tazat, the moon relents at last *(opposite)*. Pictures like this don't just happen. Advance study of astronomical data – date and time of moonrise, moonrise compared to twilight, moonrise azimuth, compass bearing, position in relation to the chosen peak ... and all too often the moon played games and hid behind distant cloud or dust haze. Camera, long lens, tripod and Peak 1331 stood ready as I looked at my watch. 'Ah, there you are.' I said. 'Wonderful! Shukran!'

A geometric landscape and a tingle of anticipation on a chill desert morning *(left)* presages another wonderful desert day.

Short shadows, a suffocating thin haze and a high midday sun, has heat and a fearful desiccation almost seeping out of the picture *(below)* as if to show the span of climatic grip the sun has in its power. Though the message is clear, it is not enough to drain the majesty of the outcrops. As I set up the telephoto shot a magnificent moufflon, its long coat flowing, like a fine, hairy hallucination, trotted across the view leaving me frozen in amazement.

The moon. apparently serene, moves like an express train *(below)* when you are trying to take its picture. Sunsets, like this one at the 'laughing rock' north of In Salah *(left)*, seem more tolerant – though science says they are no different.

Here we go again. Compass bearings, pick your spot, cross your fingers and wait *(above)* as the sun goes down. Will the wind drop so the lens doesn't shake? Idjenoudjane, a long way south-west of Arak, a dramatic Nike-whoosh on the satellite shot, is a full-time wind-tunnel for gusty clouds of dust but occasionally gives in. Will that cloud in the east spoil it? Oh dear ... then *(above right)*. 'Ah!'

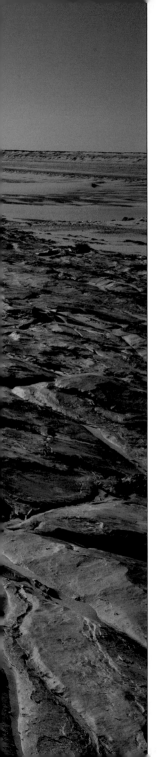

A toothed, horned wolf-gargoyle seems to wait atop bizarre, crumbling sedimentary remnants deep within the inhospitable Erg Chech south-west of Adrar (below). The erg stretches all the way down to Mauritania and comprises some of the softest, finest most treacherous sand in the Sahara. Little nobility about this wilderness – but for there to be day there must be night. At 1°W it was time to turn back. Potentially dangerous country too, south-east of Reggan (left), but a purity of form to make the intrusion memorable.

Far west

Wilderness west. 'West of what?' West of Garet el Djenoun? West of the Algiers–Tamanrasset road? West of the Tanezrouft track that heads south through Reggan to Mali? West of the Greenwich meridian? Sort of; it depends where you're looking. The large map on p.8 reminds you how big the country is. Erg Chech to Illizi is more than 1000 kilometres.

I always half-suspected Ouallene was a figment of the cartographers' imagination, a mythical joke-place dreamed-up to fill an otherwise very blank area on the map – apparently without purpose and connected to nothing. It was marked east off the already blank Tanezrouft (map, p.8 and 153). But just to the right of the vehicle in this picture and 40km farther on, Ouallene at night throbs with generators, floodlights and soldierly activity. Behind the camera it's about 360km east to the In Salah-Tamanrasset road. And 480km south-east to Tamanrasset.

The barefoot young Touareg and his camel are perfectly attuned to their stern environment – amazing and humbling to behold. But I shared his peace and contentment with the solitude, space and purity of the desert. The small erg (collection of sand dunes) 60km or so west of Adrar Ahnet (right), has crisp firm sand and this magnificent dune at its western edge.

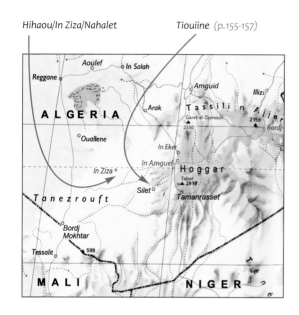

Hihaou/In Ziza/Nahalet   Tiouiine *(p.155-157)*

About half-way between the Tanezrouft route through Bordj Mokhtar and the main Tamanrasset road is the massif of Hihaou and the extraordinary guelta at In Ziza (p.74). *When I camped the night before visiting* (near left), *the full moon was almost as bright as day. To the south of Hihaou, Nahalet is north-west sentinel on the 120 mile plain stretching down to Silet. Sand on the adjoining outcrops* (opposite) *bears strange dark streaks.*

At the western end of the 190km plain is the dune-buttressed ridge at Nahalet *(left and p.152)*. Way off to the south-east are the peaks of Tiouiine *(above and next spread)* – landmarks also on the long dusty track up from the Mali border at Bordj Mokhtar.

Its dust trail hanging on the still evening air, a solitary pickup truck hurries east through the jumbled outcrops of Tiouiine along the route linking Bordj Mokhtar on the Mali border (map p.153) *with Silet and Tamanrasset among the Hoggar mountains* (next spread). *The balletic perch of some of the giant boulders* (below) *often defies probability or imagination. Visions of Indiana Jones jump to mind so if you want to photograph rocks like this it's probably best to approach quietly and select mirror-up on your SLR. Tiouiine is easier on the eye than on the tongue – the pronunciation is Tee-wy-een.*

The Hoggar

The pyramids in Egypt, the Colosseum in Rome, Monument Valley in America ... . The Hoggar mountains are Algeria's first 'must see' for many visitors and a box to tick in a tourist agency's itinerary. It is not hard to see why. But the outcrops of the Hoggar are the tip – the magnificent, jaw-dropping tip, but still just the tip – of Algeria's astonishing scenic iceberg.

Best-known and most-photographed of Algeria's landscapes (left, with peak names overleaf), the view from Père Charles de Foucauld's hermitage on Assekrem in the Hoggar – still manned by followers of the Brotherhood – is even more dramatic in its Wagnerian reality. And amongst all this gargantuan geology – tiny, perfect, delicate flowers grow among the rocks.

Camel-borne visitors concentrate on avoiding an unscheduled dismount while taking in the wild Hoggar scenery. Less often found, except by those with time to linger, are the rock-pools, minuscule streams – and the wonderous flowers and grasses that have come to rely on them.

The pedestal showing the names of the Hoggar's dramatic central area peaks *(also previous spread)* was put in position in 1939 alongside the tiny hermitage at Assekrem. Ceramic glaze ensured durability. Touareg names for peaks, valleys, plains and wadis live on also through the monumental work done in the '50s and '60s producing the Institut Géographique National 1:200k maps of the entire Algerian Sahara.

161

Ilamane (2739m) has something in common with Garet el Djenoun (p.116): its startlingly dramatic appearance and the fact it is visible (left), on the western approach to the Hoggar from a distance of 50 miles. Viewed from the south (above), its profile is slimmer and the side-lit striations are testament to the dynamics of its creation. Tahat (flat-topped mountain, centre of shot, left), is actually the highest peak in the Hoggar at 2908m but lacks Ilamane's elan.

163

Adrar Ahnet is a lozenge-shaped massif, peaks at 1420m and measures around 40 miles north-to-south. It's 'hollow' (left) – basically a multi-rim of formidable rocky hills with a single, boulder-strewn entrance (above), through a wadi on the western edge. Rain run-off favours the meagre pasture within and makes a temporary haven for Touareg livestock. A long-established well (far right), carefully covered after use, yields clear water for humans and animals alike. To the south-east by 150 miles lies Silet (map p.167). North-east is Arak, 75 miles.

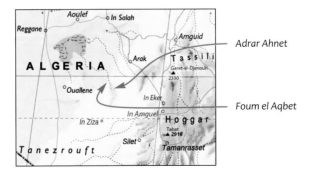

Adrar Ahnet

Foum el Aqbet

Looked at end-on from the north, the ridge at Foum el Aqbet looks little more than a mound *(left)*. But *(see picture 1 on p.228)* it's a sharp-ended spine running south five kilometres, separating Adrar Ahnet *(far left, main picture)*, from the old route to Ouallene, 120 miles west, here marked by a line of hardy yellow-flowering shrubs, probably rooted in ancient vehicle ruts and nurtured by rain that collected in them. Farther west *(above)*, closer to Ouallene, the sense of space – clean, pristine – is almost explosive.

When I awoke to another routinely magnificent Sahara dawn on the 6th of November *(above)*, I did not know that the next two or three days would be a turbulent mixture of the scary and the dramatically aesthetic. A difficult wadi, a frightening false alarm, a way out and then *(right)* ... a row of volcanic peaks, lined-up to greet me against a royal-blue sky of high wispy cirrus, the sand firm and crisp, barely registering the gentle rolling footprint of the vehicle. And ...

... after sunset, in the night, in this smoothly sanded gully, I had a visitor. The soft footprints of a lone camel strode up the rise, settled to rest not 30 yards from where I slept, and then quietly moved on north. How sad that I missed her and was unable to say hello.

The winds, the blistering sun and other agents of erosion over the millennia, bared the smooth rockface of the outcrop and then, more capriciously, arranged the hard-edged ripples of the sand ridges to catch the razor-sharp light of the late afternoon. Dawn the next morning was surreal ...

Scale *(right)*, is something perennially difficult to get a grip on in vast open spaces like the Sahara. As I headed for Tininirt *(p.85 and far left in this shot)*, peak 1076 looked like an ordinary outcrop. Up close it was different.

Peak 1076's solid rounded rump *(right)* – an especially appropriate description when viewed from certain angles – affords, with the two other outcrops in the group, enough run-off to sustain thorny acacias. Nearby, more typically conical formations *(above)*, seem to have skewered the sun on its way to the high heavens.

You can see the enticing silhouette of Izouret (above), in the distance from the Tamanrasset road, just. The sunset, ornamental high cloud and the moon (upper left), tiny in this wide-angle shot, reward the patient. A few miles farther on, a sharp spike (right), guards a bay of 'chassis-cracker' sand ridges, the final outcrop in the row and similar to the '6th November' (p.168), line-up 20 miles to the north-west.

Like so many similar structures, Issedienne's huge circular layout is best seen first on a map or satellite image. The perimeter is not complete but the outcrops are impressive – especially *(opposite)*, when the sun rises, shyly, as a cloud-masked half-circle, behind one of the lava-piles. But this is not a dead place. There seems *(left)*, to have been plenty going on in the night. And the continuous miracle of plants *(below)*, fresh and vigorous, is a source of joy and amazement.

Circular, semi-circular or arch-shaped is what Issedienne does. Right of centre in this north-to-south view *(above)*, one of the outcrops has a visual surprise for travellers *(left and next spread)*. The pasture at the fringes must be good too; the Touareg I met *(p.63)*, were bound for Issedienne.

Like the moon and high clouds at Izouret (p.178), the raven (right), at Issedienne felt obliged, for the photograph, to add artistic positioning to his natural curiosity about odd-looking vehicles in his territory. As for the arch, there were many aspects (above) to its shape.

Tesnou

Vividly portrayed on the last French maps as if the cartographers were just as moved by the peakscape as the surveyors, the Tesnou area of outcrops has the mind reeling with the technical statistics and geological origins of such a massif. Blessed with firm crisp sand – as well as some mischievous hard ridges – it's a quiet haven of calming natural beauty. With a little panache.

Due north of Issedienne by 70 miles are the peaks at Tesnou. Fringed with perfect, razor-edged sand ripples, Tesnou, as you approach, is a tantalising, mysterious massif of extraordinary shapes and formations, inviting you into its valleys and slopes. Yet you feel you want to stay 'outside' for a while to size it up. To wander within (next spread) is an awe-inspiring experience.

187

Scale again. I had seen this huge intrusion *(left)*, in the far distance. It turned out to be 30 miles before I reached it; one of Tesnou's outriders. Its smoothness and the small amount of exfoliated debris at its foot seem to attest the cataclysmic event when this single monumental addition to the landscape emerged. The head spins with statistical queries: what does it weigh? How do you define 'it'? How much heat does it soak up over a Sahara summer? When was the smooth sandy in-fill laid down? Round the corner *(above)*, a traditional peak, shored-up with sand, a gentle valley and amazing trees. But of course, *(next spread)* there's more ...

Open to the south-west *(above)* and
backing the north-east, one or two of
Tesnou's ridges, have gained smooth,
firm 'alpine' slopes of crunchy orange
sand – a kind of picnic site from which
to take in the expanses beyond. But
Tesnou also has a valley *(right)*, of
magnificent whaleback outcrops in
which grasses and acacias flourish.

The mind boggles at the geological turmoil when outcrops like this (left), were created or, say the experts, got left behind.
Not far away (above), the underfold, say geopundits, results from layering and erosion. Kitchen common-sense makes it look like a new intrusion beneath a still plastic top layer.

Huge rounded rocky outcrops abound at Tesnou *(above)*, and the nearby range named by the Touareg as Ezzouiague, born at a time when the planet was in upheaval. Despite the apparently unforgiving barrenness, wiry grass *(right)*, and tough acacias *(left)*, grow amid the gargantuan scenery. The magnificent tree on *p.88*, is quite close by and the mystery remains – when you look at the *next spread* – why (exactly why) trees, singly as a rule, appear in some places and not others.

Water (left), wind (below) and weather finessed this extraordinary and beautiful landscape once the geology produced the base material. Tesnou's outcrops are a mix of the pointed and the massively rounded; most have suffered exfoliation of the outer layers due to solar heating, cooling and cracking of the rock. Chemical action can also be a cause. When rain falls in the Sahara it is normally very heavy and enough to collect and form run-off channels even on level gravel like this. On big monoliths (next spread), mineral colouration from rain run-off is apparent. The rock below probably started with a slightly uneven lower edge but a wind venturi and sand abrasion has worn the gap to a small arch.

'No smarter veggie', I wrote in my log when I encountered this still-small lone tree *(below)*, off the edge of the Tesnou range. Certainly it had done well and chosen well and survived well. It also already had its own little colony of large red ants which, in addition to greeting visitors enthusiastically, in turn attracted small birds to take a snack from time to time: the classic tiny ecosystem that seemed to centre on every Sahara tree. The huge monolith *(right)*, called by some 'L'eléphant', on the western edge of Tesnou looms into visibility from 30 miles out. In many ways Tesnou is more spectacular than the Hoggar. Mercifully there are few signs, at present, of visitor abuse but like the rest of this area it must be scrupulously cared for and protected.

Interlude F**ractals**

Fractals
Fractals
Fractals
Fractals

A personal journey

This is not a guide book or simply a picture book. Its main *raison d'etre* is the Sahara Protected Area proposed on p.233; but it is not a production on behalf of the Algerian Government.

I have attempted to display the beauty, majesty and value of the landscapes it portrays. And to hope that someone within whose authority it lies will someday, and before it is too late, take action to protect this extraordinary part of the planet. You could argue that 'this part of the planet' is doing a pretty good job of preserving itself but there are a few important caveats to consider (as we shall see later) that could pre-empt human-kind's usual unthinking predisposition to mess things up.

Whatever other problems we as a species have to face, or have brought upon ourselves, we must not – having been blind to so much – be blind to a legacy as beautiful as the Sahara in Algeria.

This section of the book might be perceived as an indulgent personal reminiscence of landscapes and detail that epitomise, for me, the silent majesty of the Sahara. Actually that's not far off it; but it has relevance.

A memorable editorial in the American quarterly magazine *Overland Journal* by Jonathan Hanson coined a special usage of the word 'fractals'. It implied the re-examination, in greater detail, of landscape we thought we knew; often similar patterns on a smaller scale. 'Smaller bites of the world, examined more closely.' Looking closer, taking time, reveals more; enhances the value of what we see – unlike the breathless tourist groups of disparate strangers rushing from place to place sticking to a schedule.

This next section is unashamedly slow and reflective – but may convey the message with a bit more clarity. Paradoxically, a little 'anti-fractal' – seeing the great overview from space (p.208-209) – often helps.

This place (right), off the uninhabited, 275 mile, old route between Amguid and Zaouatallaz (Bordj el Haoues – map p.118 – yes, that's 275 miles), doesn't have a name, just a latitude and longitude. But with its sandy plain and almost ornamental group of conical peaks in the middle distance, I find its peace and sense of space majestic, beautiful, memorable; enough to make you catch your breath.

Even the most ordinary geological features have a simple purity about them in the tranquility of the desert. And if you 'think fractal', examine the detail, the small perfections of form are a delight to the eye and the perceptions. This (left), on the way between In Salah and Arak (map p.8), is the small plain to the south of Hassi el Kheneg and the firm, crisp dune buttresses (above) at the escarpment on its northern edge. A peaceful place to sleep under the stars and view the dawn coming up beyond the low hills to the far left of the picture.

West of Timimoun, the terrain (left) – crumbly rock, uncertain sand with the hint of soft, dangerous sebkha not far off – may set alarm bells ringing when you are vehicle-borne. But, as is often the case there is, quite nearby, some graceful natural sculpture (right) wrought by the wind to sooth the eye and brow. And, as ever, clear crisp light to flatter the contours.

Remember this (left) from page 85? It's the LandSat view of
Tininirt and a feature I could not resist going to explore. Twelve miles
long, access from the west and around the top wasn't too difficult –
albeit the route east thereafter caused a few problems. That's it again
(below) viewed from the south-east, settling down for the night. Nor could I resist, of course, ...

... taking a look at that gigantic cleft near the top. Entering from the north-east, I found the valley floor rose steadily as it headed south-westward so that, looking back, your gaze was projected to a vast clear sky to the east. And then, inevitably ... could you squeeze through the defile (right) at the western end? On foot, yes. As could – and did – wildlife over the millennia, leaving 'sheep-trails' behind them as they headed down the gullies between the rocks. An extraordinary place. I often wondered, in the spectral sort-out of the LandSat image (upper left, opposite), what caused that red colouring on the rocks along the north-eastern edge; the big rock hill on page 84 is the one and bore no clue.

Sunrise and sunset clinically constitute a twice-daily box-ticking routine that confirms the earth is still rotating as it should. But in the Sahara there is always something special about it; a seemingly infinite variety that has me rushing to the tripod amid my own equally regular routine of pushing the sleeping bag awkwardly into its stuff-sac.

A billion billion tiny dust particles hang in the sky (left) to trace the cloud-shadows as the sun puts on a dramatic display near Tazat. At Tiouiine (pron – Tee-wy-een) (right, and map p.153) the sun appears in more sober mood allowing the blues, greys and purples of the outcrops their short period of gentleness before the harsh noon renders them hostile.

Face-off. This picture (right) always makes me smile. Like a scene from a Western movie, high noon under a blistering sun and the three brave trees, damaged, bloodied but unbowed, face the implacable might of The Mountains, whose strongest fighter stands square-on to confront the heroic trio. (This is so obviously a back view of the trees as they face the looming foe!)

Less fancifully, I wondered, as I always did when seeing something like this, how these three had come to be there. The green line in the middle distance follows a shallow wadi but these, just these three, are out on the barren ground. Why here? Why three? What has afflicted two and left the other one green? And perhaps the cliffs and outcrops here around Zaouatallaz (was Fort Gardel, now Bordj el Haoues – map p.8 and 118) weren't really trying to intimidate them.

No less amazing and a continued fascination for me in a fractal kind of way (see p.202) – as the next few pages will confirm – are the Sahara's grasses (left), surviving under what seem to be impossible conditions of ceaseless desiccating wind and merciless sun. At least a tree's roots can reach down but the roots of the grasses seldom go down as much as a foot. The hardy stems, firm to the touch but topped by feathery seed-plumes that catch the sunlight, can usually manage a splash of rich green.

Toukmatine (southernmost peaks left) tops 1740m and, on a map or satellite image, juts below the south-western fringe of the Tassili n'Ajjer range of hills that stretch the 512km from Amguid in the north-west down to Djanet near the Libyan border. Accordingly it also forms a corner on the old camel – and later motorable – track between Amguid and Bordj el Haoues (maps p.8 and 118). If you're on this route going west and then north-west towards Amguid, Toukmatine lies near the edge of a featureless smooth sand sheet (below) blown off the Erg Tihodaine. It seems to say 'OK, big landmark here. Now see what you can do!' Even the map-makers gave up for a while (1:200k, IGN map, bottom right), unable to show more than a scrap of where the track was supposed to be over the sandy plain.

It was worth dallying at Toukmatine, though, and taking an exhilarating view to the south (right) – a welcome view, no doubt, for travellers coming off the black, rocky Tassili.

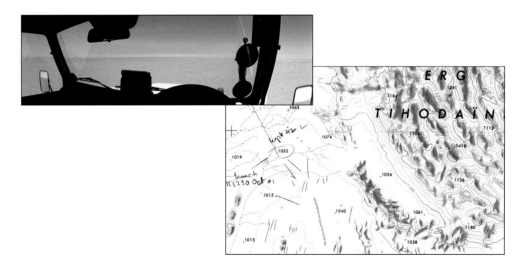

Plants probably don't respond to congratulation but these surely deserve it. Thriving in most parts of the Sahara – these were within a day and two days' drive from Toukmatine on the previous pages – the shrubs and beautiful grasses seem, at least to the non-botanist, to lead a miraculous existence. Burning sun, belting UV, almost constant wind, the absence of dew and, with a rainfall that is exceptionally rare, the plants appear robustly healthy.

Among the lower stems and roots (right), fragile but equally well-adapted desert lizards make their burrows, leaving delicate tracks in the sand as they scurry to and fro, mostly in the night, safe from predators. Seeing it all you realise a privileged view of a unique other world.

And what do messrs Darwin and Dawkins make of this? Or, specifically, our reaction to it? Is it built-in, this human sense of wonder and appreciation of beauty? And if so what might it have to do with survival of the fittest and evolution? Whilst some have it more than others, who would not be moved by this precision natural sculpture? The perfection (left) of a wind-formed ripple pattern between two rocks not far from the peak of Tazat (next spread) – a kind of classroom visual primer in aerodynamics and the trajectories of different-sized sand grains. Plus, of course, the clever plants taking shelter from the prevailing blast and doing quite nicely by the rocks. (OK, point to Darwin there.) What extraordinary discontinuity of windflow (right) could have caused this sudden change of ripple pattern at Erg Telachchimt, near Garet el Djenoun (p.116 and map p.118)? Fractal-think, looking at the detail, leaves you slow-smiling and shaking your head.

At 2061m, Tazat (above) stands a full thousand metres above the surrounding desert 30 miles or so southwest of Zaouatallaz (Bordj el Haoues, map p.8). Overlooking a wide plain to the south and a landmark visible for miles around, like Toukmatine it is a corner in the old route to Amguid. Tazat guards a skein of intriguing wadis and minor outcrops in its immediate vicinity. Where Tazat is tall, pointed and very solid, Issedienne (right, see also pp 180-185) is low and 'hollow': a roughly 15km circle of outcrops with, at one point, a characteristic geomorphology of low and hollow rocks. Among the blowholes, eroded voids and giant holes in the rocks, the foreground is strewn with super-hard translucent fragments of milky-quartz: I'd found a sea of beautiful paperweights.

'Harsh beauty' is a phrase often used to describe terrain in remote areas. Occasionally you just get 'harsh'. And the Fadnoun – between Bordj el Haoues and Illizi – majors in harsh, removing, for a while, the rose-tinted glasses and replacing them with awe at the endurance of the early camel trains, the tenacity of the road builders. Here, looking south at Falaise Sirghouine (left), 88 miles north of Bordj el Haoues, with the new road-alignment still in progress, the only way up the incline required low-range gears. The red-brown path in the picture is the new zig-zag route that will, when completed, offer a slightly less demanding slope.

The Fadnoun plateau has other surprises and this (below) is one of them – a rock pool 120 miles north of Bordj, right by the roadside. It made me want to stop and summon a hydrologist, geologist and geophysicist to explain how, in such high temperatures and shrivellingly low humidity, such a pool could survive – and where the water came from. Why did it appear so 'muddy', why was there apparently no algae (compare In Ziza on p.74)? What was the content analysis?

Taking the rough (above) with the breathtakingly smooth
(left) en route between Bordj el Haoues and Illizi (map p.8). The
hostile, crumbly rock on the Tassili (with the obligatory pair of
ravens (below) who always called to see the newcomer) clears
north of the Fadnoun plateau and Illizi to show the rich red dunes
that lie between there and the In Amenas gas fields farther on.

225

A good deal of wracking, splitting, slipping and jamming seems to have gone on (above left) at this point with a view east across the circle to Issedienne's less tortured peaks. Considerably more solid, late-afternoon sun (right) brings out the contours of my favourites at Tesnou, the more impressive for seeming to rise out of the smooth gravel plain.

Day-to-day. An aspect of the personal journey: amid all this scenic grandeur, a *modus vivendi* had to be established, a day-to-day way of living. Making the travelling work with the faithful Mercedes G-Wagen and taking great care of it – my life-line. Also being as safe as I could be in an unforgiving environment. It was all about detail and planning, not gung-ho explorer heroics. Avoiding trouble rather than blundering into it and coping with the resulting problems.

Breakfast at Foum al Aqbet (1), lunch at Aghabir (2), tea with a guest (3), dinner west of Timimoun (4). Interior packing and lash-down (5) had to be well-disciplined with the main weight (fuel and water cans) mid-wheelbase. Weight is ever the enemy so no tent – albeit the main benefit was moonlight like this (6), sleeping under the stars and waking to a delicate still dawn (7) – or the one captured for the jacket of the book.

Keeping an eye on the vehicle's well-being was paramount (8), (9), (10); and, vitally, monitoring fuel consumption (11). Well-being included, of course, recovery from soft sand when it caught me out (12) and (13). Still on overall safety, 21st century technology is worth its weight in diamonds (14) – from the left, an EPIRB (see p.237), a Thuraya satellite phone, a standby GPS and, centre, digital voice recorder for nav-log details. And navigation, naturally, was a full-time occupation, being way off-tracks in remote areas. My earliest trips were navigated using dead-reckoning and astro fixes from stars. Now we are supremely lucky to have GPS, satellite images and Google Earth. This (15) was LandSat imagery, just pre-Google Earth. Even now, though, there is no substitute for maps and dividers. The device on the window glass is a Sony short-wave radio for BBC World Service – without which I would be bereft! Another item prevented glare masking hard sand ridges which, unseen, could get a vehicle airborne. A mirror (16) reflecting sunlight onto the sand can highlight the ridge. Of course emergencies can still strike, (17): a drive-by-wire throttle failure (cause undiagnosed at the time) led to an unscheduled draining of the fuel looking for contamination.

Meanwhile, (18) the unimaginable mass of the planet rotates, slow and smooth, to give its inhabitants another glimpse of the sun (next spread) in the silent, cool of a desert dawn. The sheer flatness is a source of astonishment. If it were liquid it could surely not be flatter.

Protection

Sahara Protected Area – *L'espace des paysages*

A legacy of uncaring anarchy – mostly at the hands of western visitors. Bad enough but, despite these shots, not extensive – yet.

At the time of writing the Algerian Government is making well-judged efforts to restart the country's tourist industry. Sensibly it is turning first to its hotels infrastructure and 'set' tours for visitors. There is, or will be, the further need to address afresh the question of roaming access to the vast wilderness of the Sahara. When I first put the case for a Sahara Protected Area to the Ministry of Culture in Algiers I had mentioned that in the US National Parks, with certain provisos, you were permitted to roam on your own to enjoy the peace and solitude of the wilderness. 'This is not America!' said a smiling Mr Khalfaoui – to my undisguised delight! He was emphasising obliquely what I had already covered – my awareness (and apology) that I might be seen as another busy-body westerner telling them what to do.

But it sometimes takes another set of eyes to see things that, through familiarity, may have been missed. Especially against a background and heritage of a totally different perception: the perception of the Sahara by most, rightly over the previous few centuries, as a harsh, hostile place from which the majority took refuge.

Uniquely able to meet its fearful demands, the Sahara's majesty was probably only real to the desert professionals like the Touareg. And then to a degree taken for granted – since that was where they lived. Like the case of the Native Americans who once roamed the great plains of the US.

And even there, back then in America, in the context of his own background, it took 'another set of eyes' to see the need to protect the wilderness against the impact of westward immigrant-American expansion. In 1832 George Catlin wrote, and hoped, that 'these lands might be preserved by some great protecting policy of government ... in a magnificent park ... in all the wild and freshness of their nature's beauty.'

In Britain it was not until 1884 that James Bryce, MP, introduced the first 'freedom to roam' bill to parliament to afford public access to the countryside – a similar concept: preservation, access. The bill failed.

Looking back, it seems incredible that a further 50 years later, after the formation of leisure-activity and rural-protection groups, and despite an official inquiry in 1931 recommending a 'National Parks Authority', the British government was still being lobbied to create National Parks.

Meanwhile in America as far back as 1872 Yellowstone had, at last, been declared the world's first national park. In 1916, under President Woodrow Wilson, the Federal Government assumed state control and the nationwide concept was accepted. Just in time, it could be argued.

So should we be the ones knocking on Algeria's door to promote Sahara protection? In so far as we can look back on our own inattention, stumbling progress through the obstacles of inertia, blindness, class prejudice and vested interests, the answer – with due concern and humility – is, just maybe, yes. Or we may have some useful, if battered, opinions based on experience and a flawed history. These 'other sets of eyes' have already made the mistakes, seen the mistakes of others. Here, in a wilderness unique not just to Algeria but to the whole planet, quite a few sets of eyes recognize the Sahara's breathtaking beauty and the need to preclude the irreversible damage, both cultural and physical, that can so easily be allowed to take place with uncontrolled mass access.

• • •

In passing, 'park' (or the American 'National Monument') is surely the wrong word or phrase. Both suggest the finite, the fenced-in, the man-made; probably with an adjacent asphalt car park, ticket booth and café. 'Protected area', though equally applicable to a construction site, is functional language in English – OK for now. But this is about space. The Sahara is not, and must not be, fenced-in or enclosed. There will be an elegantly descriptive Arabic term for prime title but inevitably in Algeria French wil be applied. Clumsy in English 'the space of the landscapes', *l'espace des paysages* would serve well.

• • •

Defining a protected area is easily done. After some consultations, an hour or so in an office in the capital city with a map could well be enough. A great deal more thought, however, must be devoted to what it means, what rules and controls should apply. And then the word must be spread. The information has to be clear to those who will use it – and, not least and with sensitivity, clear to those who already live there. They must be aware, and proud, of where they live and its unique hinterland.

But first the questions. What is being protected? And what is it being protected against? The previous 200 pages gives some idea of what should be preserved and left undamaged. As mentioned on page 202, the Sahara has been preserving itself fairly effectively – and evolving gradually – for a number of millennia. Though the problem, human of course, is currently small (the present security situation keeps visitor numbers down), the signs are well established that the principal risk is careless desecration by outsiders. And, lest the spectacles become too rose-tinted, there is sometimes a certain lack of appreciation – or possibly of appropriate local infrastructure – among those native to the areas concerned. (See first picture previous page – and the whole shot, right. A situation with which we in the UK are all too familiar.)

This, though, is minor urban stuff and best dealt with by local authorities. The centre of Algiers is cleaner than the centre of London. The lesson to be learnt, and problems to be pre-empted in the *espaces des paysages*, concern the impact of excessive and undisciplined vehicular traffic in the wild remote areas. Taking the US National Parks as an example – for they do have the experience – they place a limit of six vehicles on any groups visiting a designated park area. So no rallies, no 'raids'. Not here either.

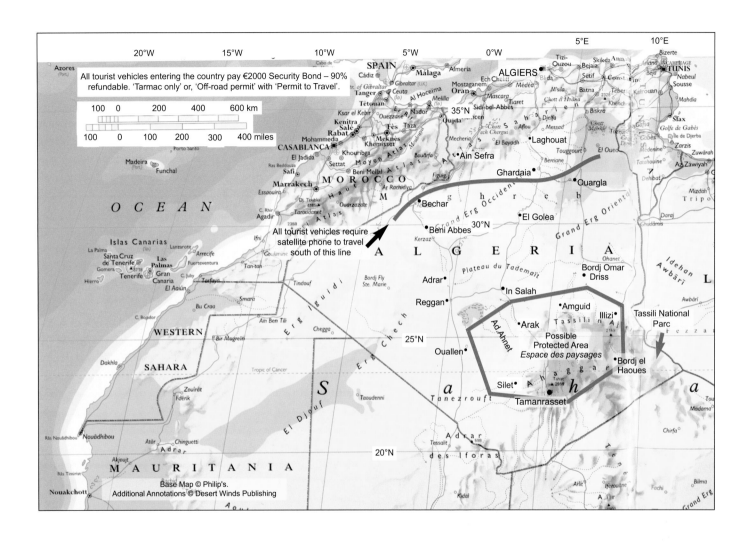

All tourist vehicles entering the country pay €2000 Security Bond – 90% refundable. 'Tarmac only' or, 'Off-road permit' with 'Permit to Travel'.

All tourist vehicles require satellite phone to travel south of this line

Possible Protected Area
Espace des paysages

Tassili National Parc

Base Map © Philip's.
Additional Annotations © Desert Winds Publishing

Sahara Protected Area – 'Espace des Paysages'.
A starting point perhaps. See next spread.

So where to start? We know what is being protected. The classic reason for keeping people out of areas like the Sahara is the 'danger'. But often just one layer down is the fear that 'the authorities' will be held responsible if visitors get into trouble. A US or UK national park is one thing, the Sahara – bigger than western Europe – is another. The urge to impose heavy-handed regulation by total banning or slipping responsibility onto 'guides' is sometimes too tempting to resist.

Better by far – and braver – is to ensure that those visiting are free to do so provided they are properly motivated, briefed, equipped – and covered. After all, no-one has banned surfing, ocean sailing, mountaineering or private flying just because it can be dangerous. Those taking part – at the behest either of common sense or regulation – have the right equipment and training before setting out. If the beauty and solitude of the Sahara are to be shared among responsible people, why should regulation there be any different?

The sequence of ensuring control, safety, and environmental care, then evolves itself. Many formats are possible but one basis for visitor vehicle import and regulation is shown opposite and below.

1. **The Security Bond.** A substantial sum - maybe €1500 – levied, at visa-application stage, on foreign visitors planning to visit in their own vehicles. It would be 90% refundable on departure from the country in the absence of any incident requiring rescue or breach of protected area rules (see opposite). A flat fee according to area is a possible alternative.

2. **Equipment level, Permit to Travel.** At visa-application stage minimum equipment levels according to the area to be visited would be made clear and the visa applicant would sign as intending to comply. Actual compliance would be checked at the port of entry. According to area, on- or off-tracks, this list would include a satellite phone, EPIRB (Emergency Position-Indicating Radio Beacon) as used by yachtsmen, fuel and water reserves. The provisional Permit to Travel, issued with the visa would be validated according to 'Tarmac only' or 'Off-road' category at port of entry after vehicle and equipment inspection by port officials.

3. **Guides.** Visitors on a first – or any other – visit would be advised to take guides or travel with tour operators. Here, responsibility for safety rests with the tour operator. But the most precious and unique feature of the Sahara is the space, solitude and time to linger that it affords visitors, should they wish to travel on their own at their own pace. As for ocean sailors at sea, this right must be preserved at all costs. The temptation to over-legislate regarding guides and convoys should be avoided. Many current 'guides' are in fact only drivers whose knowledge is limited to their own area; their aim all too often is simply to rush at high speed from A to B and many are unable even to read maps.

4. **Environment – physical and cultural.** Low-impact tourism should be the aim – both physically and culturally. Exposure to cheap western tourism and to insensitive tourists has spoiled Tunisia and resulted in irreversible cultural degradation in some regions. Western tourists do not own the world nor have they the right to establish a mono-culture. A national policy of up-market, high-value, low-volume tourism would be enormously beneficial. As a validating snapshot of this viewpoint, the contrast between tourist-saturated Tunisia and hitherto isolated Libya in 1998 was very marked – and much in Libya's favour.

• • •

Implementing a Protected Area scheme such as proposed here could easily result in bureaucratic excess that precludes the enjoyment of the very qualities uniquely offered by a visit to the Sahara – the peace and solitude and the beauty of the landscape. Keeping the regulations as simple as outlined opposite and, above all, making sure that visitors are aware of them right from the start, is essential.

The proposals are demanding but simple and will preserve cultural values as well as the ability of visitors to enjoy the priceless qualities that only the real desert can offer. They will ensure that only well-motivated outsiders go to the Sahara. They will ensure too that these visitors are well prepared and respectful of their pristine surroundings and respectful of the people whose country and culture it is.

Simplicity encapsulated – discuss ...

It could be as simple as this. Control, clarity, safety. A possible regulatory structure for visitors to the protected area. A multi-lingual version of this, together with notes similar to those opposite would be shown on Algerian Consulate websites and given to visitors applying for visas.

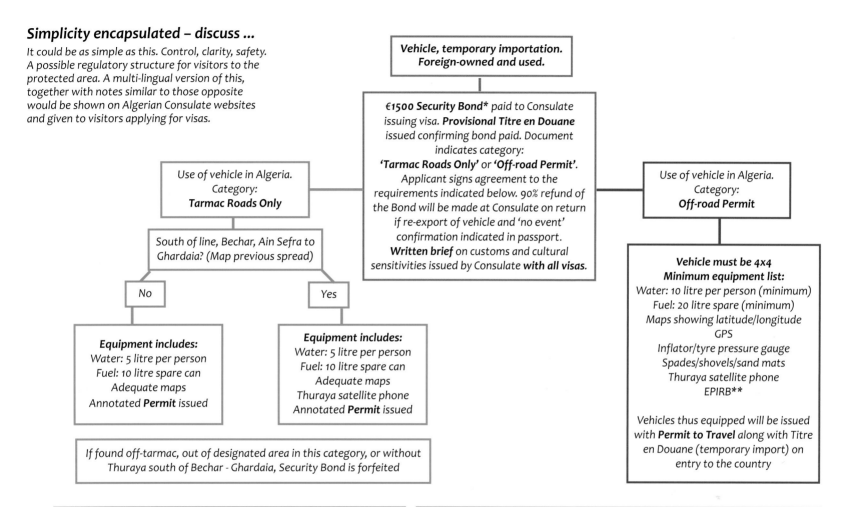

Vehicle, temporary importation. Foreign-owned and used.

€1500 Security Bond paid to Consulate issuing visa. **Provisional Titre en Douane** issued confirming bond paid. Document indicates category:*
'Tarmac Roads Only' *or* **'Off-road Permit'.** *Applicant signs agreement to the requirements indicated below. 90% refund of the Bond will be made at Consulate on return if re-export of vehicle and 'no event' confirmation indicated in passport.* **Written brief** *on customs and cultural sensitivities issued by Consulate* **with all visas.**

Use of vehicle in Algeria. Category:
Tarmac Roads Only

South of line, Bechar, Ain Sefra to Ghardaia? (Map previous spread)

No

Yes

Equipment includes:
Water: 5 litre per person
Fuel: 10 litre spare can
Adequate maps
Annotated **Permit** *issued*

Equipment includes:
Water: 5 litre per person
Fuel: 10 litre spare can
Adequate maps
Thuraya satellite phone
Annotated **Permit** *issued*

If found off-tarmac, out of designated area in this category, or without Thuraya south of Bechar - Ghardaia, Security Bond is forfeited

Use of vehicle in Algeria. Category:
Off-road Permit

Vehicle must be 4x4
Minimum equipment list:
Water: 10 litre per person (minimum)
Fuel: 20 litre spare (minimum)
Maps showing latitude/longitude
GPS
Inflator/tyre pressure gauge
Spades/shovels/sand mats
Thuraya satellite phone
EPIRB**

Vehicles thus equipped will be issued with **Permit to Travel** *along with Titre en Douane (temporary import) on entry to the country*

---

*Security Bond. The purpose of the Security Bond is a form of insurance to contribute towards any assistance or rescue activities from the Algerian authorities should this arise. If there are no incidents then the refund of 90% of the amount paid is made. A substantial bond of this kind will also ensure that visitors realise the importance of using a properly equipped vehicle, operating it correctly and observing the Travel Regulations and Visitors Code of Conduct in the Saharan regions.

**EPIRB = Emergency Position-Indicating Radio Beacon. This is a small item about 15 cm long of the type routinely carried by small sea-going boats, registered in the user's name with the national Coastguard, When triggered, it transmits a radio signal on 121.5 MHz or 406 MHz which is picked up by satellites on the world-wide marine rescue network and linked to the user's registration. The position of the transmission is also transmitted so rescue can be easily directed. EPIRB would be used only for extreme emergencies. Thuraya would be used for serious but not dire problems.

By the same author

Vehicle-dependent Expedition Guide, Edn 2.1   ISBN 978-0-9532324-4-4
Four-by-four Driving   ISBN 978-0-9532324-3-7
Quiet for a Tuesday   ISBN 978-0-9532324-5-1
          Details and extracts: *www.desertwinds.co.uk*

Desert Winds

The small print

First published in the United Kingdom in 2010 by
Desert Winds Publishing, 44 Salusbury Lane, Hertfordshire SG5 3EG, England

Written, illustrated, and designed by Tom Sheppard, MBE
Text, photographs, artwork, design and layout copyright © Tom Sheppard 2010
Maps reproduced by kind permission of Philip's

The moral right of Tom Sheppard to be identified as the author of this work has been asserted in accordance with the Copyright, Designs and Patents Act of 1988.

A CIP catalogue record for this book is available from the British Library.
ISBN 978-0-9532324-6-8

Printed and bound (in 12pp sections) by Printer Trento S.r.l, Italy
Typeface: Main text – Tiepolo Book 9 on 13 pt (pp 203-231 Orange Std 9.5 on 13 pt)
          Captions – Candara Italic 8 on 10 pt
Illustrations: High definition stochastic (screenless) printing

Acknowledgement and heartfelt thanks

My thanks for the kindness and hospitality of the Algerians I met and the tolerance of the Touareg out in the desert for whom I have boundless admiration. My gratitude for the ability to recognise the beauty of elemental wild places and their attendant plant and animal life – and the hope that I may be able to communicate it in some way to others.

But there would have been no book at all without the unsung wizards and digital technorati at Apple Computer, QuarkXPress (Quark 8.12), Adobe (Photoshop CS4, Bridge and Camera Raw 5.2) software. And I make no apology for repeating the praise here as I did in *Quiet for a Tuesday*. Heroes all – careful, meticulous heroes; may they prosper, sup wine and peel grapes to a contented old age and garner richly deserved satisfaction for their contributions to what we see and read every day, worldwide. These are people our dumb media like to label as nerds and geeks; but these are people, like thousands of skilled technical folk, who actually do something from which we all benefit. They deserve more recognition.